ABC

African Instruments

AFRICA is the second largest continent in the world. It contains 54 countries, has at least 7 major rivers and mountain ranges, and is home to the world's largest desert, The Sahara. Over 1 billion people live here, speaking over 2,000 languages between them! It is the birthplace of mankind.

Across Africa, music and dance are used every day for communication and in cultural events. Traditional African music is diverse and has influenced many other types of music. As African people have moved around the world their music has always accompanied them. For example, millions of enslaved Africans were taken to The Americas during the Atlantic Slave Trade. We can hear many types of music across The Americas that contain characteristics of African music.

This book provides an exciting introduction to some of the many traditional musical instruments from around the African continent.

AFRICA
Mediterranean Sea
TUNISIA
MOROCCO
ALGERIA
LIBYA
EGYPT
WESTERN SAHARA
MAURITANIA
MALI
NIGER
CHAD
SUDAN
Red Sea
ERITREA
DJIBOUTI
Gulf of Aden
CAPE VERDE
SENEGAL
GAMBIA
GUINEA-BISSAU
GUINEA
BURKINA FASO
NIGERIA
CÔTE-D'IVOIRE
GHANA
TOGO
BENIN
SIERRA LEONE
LIBERIA
CAMEROON
CENTRAL AFRICAN REPUBLIC
SOUTH SUDAN
ETHIOPIA
SOMALIA
EQUATORIAL GUINEA
SAO TOME AND PRINCIPE
GABON
CONGO
UGANDA
RWANDA
KENYA
DEMOCRATIC REPUBLIC OF THE CONGO
BURUNDI
UNITED REPUBLIC OF TANZANIA
INDIAN OCEAN
SEYCHELLES
ATLANTIC OCEAN
ANGOLA
ZAMBIA
MALAWI
COMOROS
MOZAMBIQUE
MADAGASCAR
MAURITIUS
ZIMBABWE
BOTSWANA
NAMIBIA
SWAZILAND
SOUTH AFRICA
LESOTHO

HOW TO USE THIS BOOK:

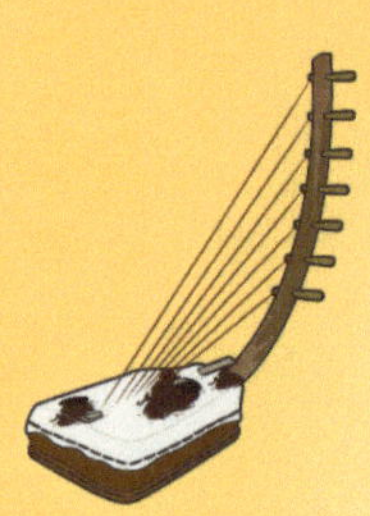

1. CHOOSE A LETTER **A**

2. DISCOVER THE INSTRUMENT

3. SEE HOW IT IS PLAYED 

4. FIND OUT MORE USING THE FACT BUBBLES

Who / Where

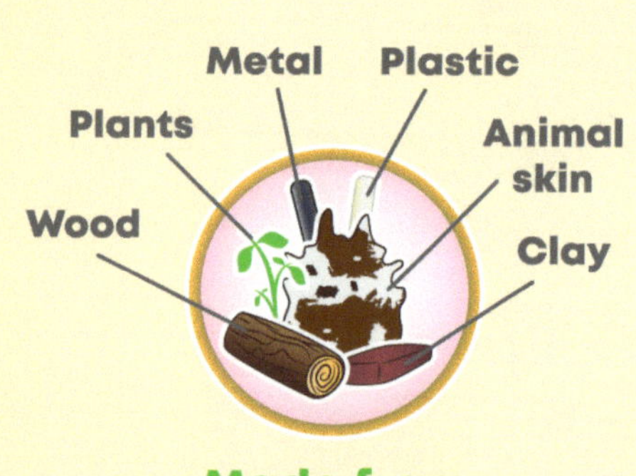

Made from

The Adungu is a type of arched harp which makes a sound when the strings are plucked

Additional Information

Musical family

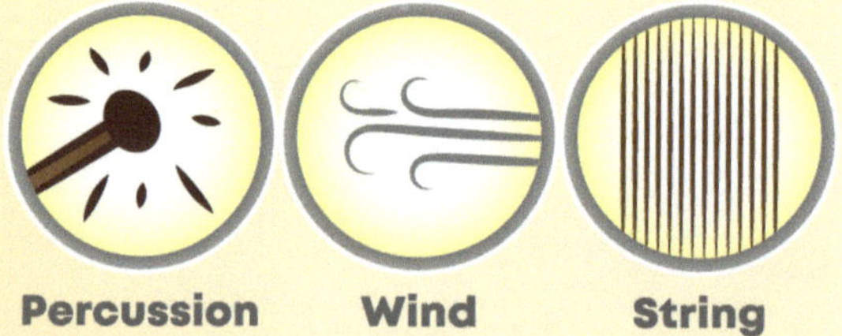

1. Letter
2. Instrument
A is for ADUNGU
The Adungu is a type of arched harp which makes a sound when the strings are plucked
It comes in various sizes, with up to 10 strings
UGANDA
4. Fact bubbles
3. How it is played

A is for
ADUNGU

The Adungu is a
type of arched harp
which makes a sound
when the strings
are plucked.

It comes in
various sizes,
with up to 10
strings.

UGANDA

B is for
BALAFON

The Balafon is
a type of
xylophone.

The wooden keys
are struck for
sound.

MALI

C is for
CALABASH

The Calabash is a
vine plant which
bears a fruit used to
make many different
African instruments.

The Calabash Rattle,
Kora, Balafon and
Cabasa are just some
of the musical
instruments made
using this fruit.

ACROSS
AFRICA

D is for
DUNDUN

The animal skin covering the drum is hit with a stick to make sound.

The Dundun is a "talking drum" which can mimic the tone of human voices.

Mande People
WEST AFRICA

E is for
EKWE

The Ekwe is a wooden drum with rectangular holes in its body.

The player uses a wooden stick to beat the drum, traditionally to communicate with people far away.

Igbo People
NIGERIA

F is for
FONTOMFROM
The Fontomfrom is a tall drum played by the Ashanti people.
It is often played during royal celebrations.
Ashanti People
GHANA

G is for GOJE
The Goje is a type of one or two stringed fiddle, played with or without a bow.
It is made from a hollowed-out plant covered in snake or lizard skin. The string is made from animal hair.
People in the SAHEL REGION

H is for
HOSHO
The Hosho are a type of rattle played mainly by Shona people.
They are made from hollowed out plants and have seeds inside them.
ZIMBABWE

I is for IGBA
The Igba is the name of the drum family played by the Igbo people.
Igba drums have a variety of shapes and can be up to 3 feet tall.
Igbo People
NIGERIA

J is for
JEMBE

It is mostly played by men using their bare hands.

The Jembe is a goblet-shaped wooden drum that makes a loud sound when struck.

WEST AFRICA

K is for
KORA
The Kora
is a stringed
harp-like
instrument.
It is often
played by musical
storytellers,
known as 'Jalis'.
WEST
AFRICA

L is for LAMELLOPHONE

You can find many types of Lamellophones throughout Africa.

They have a series of metal tongues that are plucked to make musical sounds.

ACROSS AFRICA

M is for
MOLIMO

The Molimo trumpet is often played by Bambuti pygmy during their rituals and events.

It can be made from metal, wood or bamboo.

D.R. of CONGO

N is for
NYATITI

The Nyatiti
is a stringed
instrument
which is plucked
to make music.

Traditionally,
the player wears
metal bells on their
right leg and a metal
ring on their big toe
to accompany the
Nyatiti-playing.

KENYA

O is for OJA FLUTE

The Oja Flute is made of wood and usually has engravings.

In dance festivities you will often see the Oja Flute being played.

NIGERIA

P is for
PREMPENSUA

The Prempensua is a large wooden box lamellophone.

The player sits on top of the box to play it.

GHANA

Q is for
QRAQEB

They are normally made of metal or wood.

The Qraqeb are a castanet-like instrument played to create distinct rhythms.

NORTH AFRICA

R is for RASP

There are many types of Rasps played in Africa.

A stick is rubbed across the notched body to produce sound.

S is for SOGO

The Sogo is a barrel drum played by the Ewe people.

It can be played with hands or sticks.

T is for
TAMBIN

The Tambin is
a wooden flute
played by the
Fulani people.

It is made
from a vine
that grows in
West Africa.

Fulani People
WEST
AFRICA

U is for
UDU

The Udu is an instrument of the Igbo people that is struck to make sound.

It originated as a water vessel and is normally made of clay.

Igbo People
NIGERIA

V is for
VUVUZELA
The modern Vuvuzela is a colourful plastic horn producing one musical note.
It is often played very loudly by football fans during matches.
SOUTH AFRICA

W is for WASAMBA

The Wasamba
Rattle consists of
a wooden handle
supporting
a row of discs.

When it is
shaken it makes
a sound similar
to a hand clap.

WEST
AFRICA

X is for
XALAM
The Xalam is a wooden stringed instrument.
It is often played by singing storytellers known as "Griots".
WEST AFRICA

Y is for YABARA

It is mostly played by women in Mali.

The Yabara is a shaker made from a hollowed out plant and strings of beads that cover it.

MALI

Z is for ZUKRA
The Zukra is a type of bagpipe made using animal skin and horns.
It is often played at social events such as weddings and funerals.
LIBYA

For Nur